My Sh Words

Consultants

Ashley Bishop, Ed.D.

Sue Bishop, M.E.D.

Publishing Credits

Dona Herweck Rice, *Editor-in-Chief*

Robin Erickson, *Production Director*

Lee Aucoin, *Creative Director*

Sharon Coan, *Project Manager*

Jamey Acosta, *Editor*

Rachelle Cracchiolo, M.A.Ed., *Publisher*

Image Credits

cover Eric Isselée/Shutterstock; p.2 Hasan Serdar Çelik/IStockphoto; p.3 Brian Goodman/Shutterstock; p.4 Amriphoto/iStockphoto; p.5 Melissa King/Shutterstock; p.6 Darrensharvey/Dreamstime; p.7 Jeecis/Dreamstime; p.8 Eric Isselée/Shutterstock; p.9 Eltoro69/Dreamstime; p.10 Mushakesa/Shutterstock; back cover Mushakesa/Shutterstock

Teacher Created Materials

5301 Oceanus Drive
Huntington Beach, CA 92649-1030
http://www.tcmpub.com

ISBN 978-1-4333-3987-5

© 2012 Teacher Created Materials, Inc.

Printed in Malaysia
THU001.50393

Here is a **sh**oe.

Is a **sh**oe here?

Here is a **sh**irt.

Is a **sh**irt here?

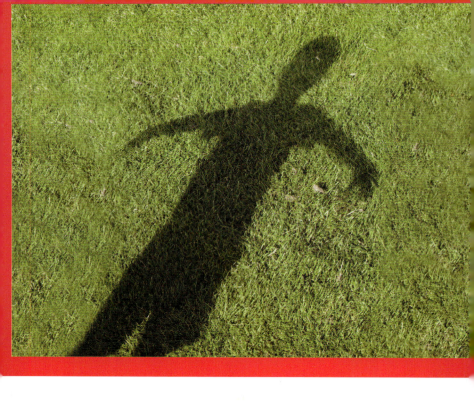

Here is a **shadow**.

Is a **sh**adow here?

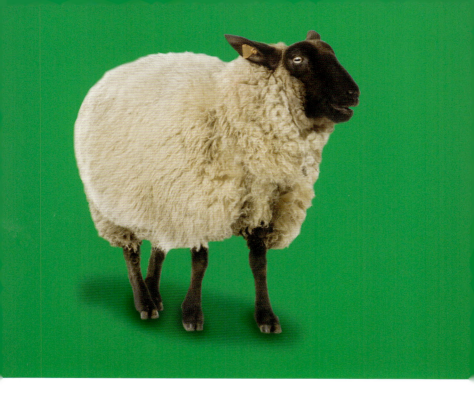

Here is a **sh**eep.

Is a **sh**eep here?

Here are shells.

Glossary

shadow

sheep

shells

shirt

shoe

Sight Words

Here   is   a   are

Activities

- Read the book aloud to your child, pointing to the *sh* words. Help your child describe where the *sh* objects are found.
- Look for a sign that reads, NO SHOES, NO SHIRT, NO SERVICE. Have your child find the sh words.
- Find the sheep at a petting zoo. Touch their fleece and talk about how it is used to make wool sweaters and blankets.
- Read the story *A House for Hermit Crab* to your child. Look at shells if you have a collection.
- Help your child think of a personally valuable word to represent the letters *sh*, such as *shake*.